Richard Meier

Richard Meier
Recent Works

Edited by
Silvio Cassarà

Universe

Design
Marcello Francone

Editorial Coordination
Luca Molinari

Editing
Marta Cattaneo

Layout
Paola Ranzini

Translations
Catherine Bolton for Globe Srl

First published in the United States of America in 2004 by
Universe Publishing
A Division of Rizzoli International Publications, Inc.
300 Park Avenue South
New York, NY 10010

www.rizzoliusa.com

Originally published in Italy in 2004 by
Skira Editore S.p.A.
Palazzo Casati Stampa
via Torino 61
20123 Milano
Italy

www.skira.net

© 2004 by Skira editore

2004 2005 2006 / 10 9 8 7 6 5 4 3 2 1

ISBN 0-7893-1222-0

Library of Congress Catalogue Control Number 2004110349

Printed in Italy

Index

Richard Meier and architecture as a privileged place
Silvio Cassarà

One of the most fascinating aspects of Richard Meier's architectural journey is the sheer brevity of his training period and the corresponding debut of riveting works.

In the period between 1961 and 1965, after designing just three buildings (in reality one-family houses) and several interiors, the advent of the Smith House identifies a strategy that, following the Darien debut, would remain precisely that – an approach absolutely consistent with the principles of this first project. In essence, this strategy was simply allowed then to perfect itself or evolve, and all this occurred without the "progressive"steps typical of the youthful phases of any architect.

The scheme of opposite components poised in equilibrium (simple-complex, structure-form) – of "memory" understood also as invention, of design experienced as an absolute process of juxtaposing art and technique – is asserted in the Smith House in all the concentrated potential of the house-object, a finished structure that is also a prototype.

Here, colorlessness – white – as well as structure and materials manifest situations that imply relationships of non-contamination seemingly universal and acontextual, linked to the absolutism of a process that is perfect and, above all, perfectible, in both ideal and execution.

Most surreal and magical – and the reason it is difficult to imitate except by cloning – is the very fact that it was built.

Richard Meier's architecture has followed these fundamentals to the present day.

His limited apprenticeship thus exploded in a house manifesto whose construction showed the feasibility of a powerfully cultured, theoretical and ambitious conceptual program uniting the "Five Architects." Meier led this group through an examination of constructed works toward the ultimate confrontation with a pragmatism and reality from which the others, by virtue of their backgrounds, seemed far removed. This essentially arose when overly profound historicised *recherche* polemically sterilized the underpinnings of one of America's totems, the one-family house, reinterpreting it from a Modernist slant but not a serialized one.

Real and accidental affinities[1] formed the platform of a partnership that would be overturned not only by the profession itself but also by the evolution of the same research, converging at the crossroads between Graves's return to Classicism and the continuity of the group's frontier Modernism. Richard Meier, like the others, however, continued to investigate these issues on a residential scale, a size which facilitated control (still tactical) over "systems set in relation to each other," as mentioned above. Here, however, these systems were applied by stripping away the excesses of Eisenman's conceptual structuralism and Hejduk's symbolism. As to purism, it was the true binding element, the factor uniting them all.

Geometric rigor, augmented by the incisiveness of colorlessness – essential for creating a psychological aura – was the first stage in a program manifesting the link between artistic process and its intrinsic abstraction (the first plans for the Atheneum are a good example) and the archetypes of Modernist memory. By now, this memory was so firmly entrenched in the United States that its deepest roots – Miesian concepts (and post-Johnson) clearly cherished by Richard Meier – were already being disputed.

An imaginary debut in Los Angeles would have diluted this house in the infinity of a boundless and shimmering urban landscape. On the East Coast, however, this structure emphasized the creation of a privileged area of intervention, with an exactitude – that of culture – acquiring a value that, didactically, is quasi-polemical and symbolic in scope. It is conceptually similar to the Guggenheim's impact on Fifth Avenue: a unique situation – but is it really? – of convergence of two philosophical conceptions that are far removed yet similar in the metaphysical abstraction of their outcome.

Nonetheless, Meier closely studied Wright's philosophy evident in Atlanta's High Museum of Art. The latter likewise confirms the scope of his study of historic memories "by types" reflected by the Museum's architecture, which aspires to forge closer parallels with the cityscape, as opposed to Meier's first projects, almost all of which were residential. These are the parallels that the historic cities of Europe – chiefly German ones – would provide in the various competitions that Meier entered and, in many cases, won.

In effect, the key to interpreting the entire anthology of Richard Meier's architecture lies in what occurred during this period *vis-à-vis* spatial settings, which were quite limited for the most part. Meier always delved further into this research, marked by preset ideal objectives and results requiring verification in a highly specific setting.

The input differs: the problem of non-relationship (to wit, the relationship) with the exterior, the internal-external problem, the structure or rather the problem of tectonics. Meier's architecture is composed of objects that are magnificently "lost" in their setting, regardless of their scale and exterior.

It is the *solitude* (indispensable above all) of the Smith House, the rigor of Twin Parks, the sequence of aligned houses for Berlin (unfortunately never built), but it is also the project for Naples, Ulm and the sprawling Getty campus in the Hollywood hills.

With any system that is studied, the more abstract and unrelated it is to its surroundings, urban or non-urban, the more valid it is from a design standpoint.

This architecture highlights the terms of incompatibility between the architecture of the past and modern architecture, at least as far as dialectical contamination is concerned. Likewise, it acts at the level of direct comparison mediated by geometric relations, entrusting the results to the process of streamlining the relationships between historic matrices with an intrinsic and mathematical value.

Actually, the isolation and extraneousness of the forms are a bridge to the continuity of the inequalities comprising urban polyphony. In the case of numerous works in historic centers, the form is regulated by the mathematical angle of the grids on which functional abstraction is implanted. The more customary forms are deracinated – Ulm, for example, with a circular white volume set against the vertical thrust of the cathedral – the more effective the layout with respect to the rare projects in which the architect attempts mediation.

Consequently, the constancy of the instruments being used represents an implicit axiom of intrinsically valid results.

The Smith House thus ushered in a design phase of unsuspected scope, chiefly because it was ostensibly oriented towards investigating the specificity of apparent mnemonic recovery, the "nostalgia" of Tafuri's memory.[2] But the path was opened, becoming a "system."

Just two years later, the Saltzman House reconfirmed this focus on powerfully plastic architecture and a more sophisticated play of opposites (empty-full, static-dynamic, frontal-rotated). This interplay was effectively achieved with a square plan, balanced by the unavoidable presence of the annex of the low body and by the connection accentuating the seamless continuity between interior and exterior space. Meier is not generally fond of colliding volumes, and here very few actually do. The volumes of the Saltzman House are clearly defined, and they make the functional organization easily discernable from the exterior; the enormous slash of the living room also provides a glimpse of the fluidity of the interior, revealing the value given to the rapport between structure and enclosure, as well as their autonomous and complementary natures. These two interdependent variables become fundamental throughout the subsequent path.

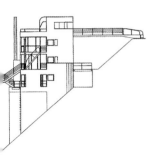

Moreover, this approach thrusts the open portions of the living areas toward the edge of the horizon. The very same concept was used at the Douglas House, which is anchored between the trees of a magnificent slope in Michigan with a sheer drop to the lake, in a "dialogue" with infinity. The layout is the same as the Smith House, including the outside stairs. Abstraction is accentuated by the location and by the suggestion of the structure's use, in crossing, conquering and possessing the house in its entirety by means of ramps, stairs and dizzying paths over nothingness. Wright immediately comes to mind.

At Bear Run, the house on the waterfall, one must walk outside to access the guesthouse, and at Harbor Springs, the fireplace-sculpture gives an aesthetic penchant to the role played by the omnipresent rituality of Wright's fireplace. However the Douglas House touches the soil just enough to anchor itself and project a landing pier.

Similar roles are interpreted in a way that is also psychologically alternative; while the Kaufman House is a tangible object visible from all sides, the Douglas House is designed for privileged views from the air or water.

Meier brings to the lake a universal, urban layout: white, technological and perfectly pristine. Melville replaces Whitman.

The project is dated 1971, one year after the plans for the Bronx Developmental Center (completed in 1977). The latter ushered in the phase of metal cladding panels, used for a hospital-like clinical asserting autonomy and urban articulation at the very edge of an important suburban roadway.

Thus, in the early Seventies the research field and its objectives were clearly defined in the completed projects. Just one piece was missing, and it involved the "technical" variable. The fine-tuning of a complete cladding system, entailing the use of metal panels, appeared in a series of projects that were never built. Subsequently applied at the Bronx, this system blossomed with the Atheneum, an architecture inconceivable with any other façade. Yet it goes beyond this. The system effectively prevents any sort of intrusion or imperfection in execution. At the same time, it also makes it possible to increase the import of each intervention, as revealed by the drawings for the Atheneum, done on an ocher background that enhances its surreal role.

Above all, however, it becomes clear that metal paneling, progressing from the rectangular subdivision used at the Bronx to the squared layout, cannot help but influence the perceptual and organizational system of new projects. And it is the only system capable of interpreting and becoming compatible – in short, identifying itself – with formally complex architectures drawn from intentionally interrupted geometries: circumferences, squares, straight lines.

By eliminating wood siding (all the early works were faced with wooden planks simply painted, as was common practice for all houses in New England and elsewhere) for the use of metal and stone, the panels must necessarily be applied three-dimensionally, in a way that redefines the overall space rather than acting simply as facing. Otherwise, the works would unravel into the serial format of prefab buildings. Given the groundwork here, however, this is unimaginable, and it is a device that Isozaki alone managed to use with the same kind of energy at Gumma.

The incisiveness of Meier's buildings is tied to the ideal three-dimensional "depth" of this technique, which encloses the columns of the Atheneum and the buttresses of the High Museum. It lends itself perfectly to following supple lines and curved walls, underscoring their solidity and altering their gravity. It is also one of the prime instruments for varying the perceived and basic systems of the abstraction observed in this architecture. Here, the iteration and monotony of the system, an undifferentiated grid, is transformed by its flexibility to redefine unusual formal systems (the volumes of the entrance to the High Museum, for example).

Structure, cladding and form are interdependent. And they are subject to variations and intrinsic evolutions that, by virtue of their basic geometry, ensure the compositional coherence that is yet another distinctive element of Meier's architecture. Because they are interdependent, however, these three systems take on loftier meanings and values, ones beyond autonomy and function.

Thus the structural system is simultaneously the bearing and architectural system, and the cladding absorbs technical data as well as mnemonic information and allusions.

Memory and mechanical suggestions become leverage for this design concept, capable of merging and reinterpreting Modernism in a contemporary light.

While Meier's debut projects established an ideological layout through a complex compositional arrangement, chiefly involving isolated buildings, museums and homes, in the Eighties he expanded the scale. Nonetheless, his later projects continue to hark back to previous contexts. The Hartford Seminary, the Ackerberg House and even the Westchester House point to several strategies that were adopted and reinterpreted in urban settings. The Westchester House is a test of lines of force as plan generators, and the Hartford Seminary and Ackerberg House mark urban installations on a reduced scale that are rediscovered in Europe (Canal Plus, Hilversum, Schwendi). Again, solidity of volume is rejected for its elaboration in a sequential view, as at the Swissair Building in Melville. The planes serve to highlight the depth of the plan generators (as at Barcelona or the Jean Arp Museum) that are extended beyond the covered area, as is the rigor of the skylights that mark out the internal routes. Then there is the Rachofsky House, a masterpiece of "alluded" space leading to a definite volume – the parallelepiped – that is destroyed and then reassembled in partitions and plate glass that acquire uncommon depth. If anything, the novelty lies in the autonomy claimed by these partitions in the overall process. The staircase is relative. And Meier,[3] in his somewhat rare comments on his own architecture, is fond of emphasizing the territorial vocation of his works. This starts with the way the High Museum contaminates the city, piercing the grid of the site with the entrance niche, and moves to the mathematical dialogues, through grids, between old and new at the Frankfurt Museum. It continues with the passkey of focal perspectives at the Getty Center, grafted onto the diagrams of "reason" – shifted, rotated by three and a half degrees – or *ratio* that, precisely because it is altered by poetic intrusion, remains the founding template of this architecture.

It is *ratio* that releases function from forms tautologically accepted as such (the wings of the double-cantilever roof of the Neugebauer House, to

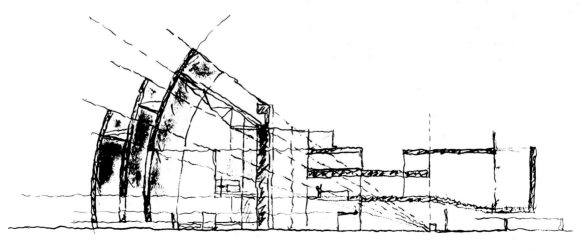

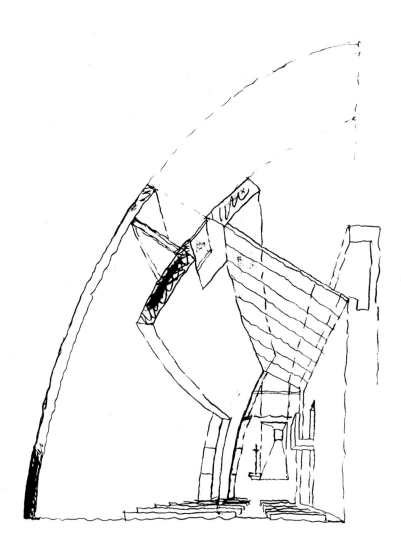

The church of the Year 2000 Rome

7 March 1996

cite one of the most recent examples), justifying their meaning and function. Another example can be found in the webs of the Jubilee Church, whose geometric genesis is persistently emphasized.

The organization of *ratio* can be credited with controlling the relative complexities pertaining to this architecture. This culminates in results that are ultimately reassuring because of this blend of technique, materials and radiance, and because of the reestablished link with the history of building. These results are reconciled by Meier's evident pleasure of knowing how to create spaces, no matter what, and by his use of tectonics to express anti-tectonic concepts,[4] elaborating formal patterns to be subjected to the absolute control of details and to the equally absolute lack of reticence in manifesting historical sources and references. And this is precisely what happens, regardless of what these references may be. The wall of La Tourette reappearing in various projects, the façade of the Pavilion "L'Esprit Nouveau", the industrial metal staircases set against a wall – the latter being a Meier creation – are all turned into archetypes. They become incorporated into the current vocabulary of an architecture that unfolds and is acknowledged in the value of its formal choices, eliminating even the significance of furniture. Only furnishings with value and architectural rigor are used, such as those of Le Corbusier or Aalto. In the case of specially designed items, interior design is interpreted along Secession or even Shaker lines, reintroducing shades of romanticism anticipated by the "lightened" reinterpretation of Wright's windows, in the North Salem house. The inherent value of memory filters down to the details. Indeed, an intervention by Frank Stella was attempted for the Giovannitti House, an incredible interplay of solid "volumes" – and with Meier, even windows flaunt this trait – in a small house in Pennsylvania.

This experimentation into the forms of reason – the circle or the straight line – can nonetheless provide stable solutions and an architecture recognizable to a society in motion, induced to grasp fragments of emotion and a patch of sky along ramps, stairs and paths that lend fluidity to extraordinarily controlled interiors and white exteriors. There is no metaphor here. The most recent architectures are merely larger and ceremonial, but they are always perfectly identifiable and traceable to the known layout.

Abstraction is indeed ubiquitous. As Peter Eisenman commented in presenting his project for House VI[5], architecture is based on the dialectic of the real and the virtual.

Architecture is the synthesis of the transcendental condition arising from this dialectic. And it is precisely what occurs in nearly all the elegant, cultured, white architectures of Richard Meier.

[1] K. Frampton, *Storia dell'Architettura contemporanea*, Zanichelli Editore, 1993, p. 368.

[2] *Les bijoux indiscrets*, Introduction by M. Tafuri to "Five Architects NY." Officina Editore. C. Izzo and A. Gubitosi.

[3] K. Frampton, *Richard Meier*, Electa, 2003, pp. 186-191.

[4] *Richard Meier*, Academy Editions. St. Martin's Press, p. 31.

[5] *Progressive Architecture*, June 1977; *Peter Eisenman on House VI*, p. 59.

Works

The Atheneum
New Harmony, 1975–79

The Atheneum represents the fusing of experimentation in the visual arts with the architect's construction program. This is facilitated – but also rendered difficult in this case – by the elusive function of the building (celebratory architecture in the broadest sense) and the possibility of intervening on a sweeping scale with the unconditional use of total space.

Isolated from the town and abounding in evocative views (e.g. the approach by boat when the nearby river floods), the Atheneum lends itself perfectly to a three-dimensional interpretation with a cubist slant. It has thus been elevated to assume values and architectural functions in an environment that ceaselessly changes visually, because it is based on the principle of movement.

Both the internal and external viability have adopted this principle, incorporating metaphorical fragments and structural medleys in their viewpoints.

The architecture also celebrates the ramp as a prime element of composition. Likewise, it marks the definitive regularization of design stratagems (the skylight routes, the coincidence of structural and ideal systems, the structure, itineraries, program, site and, above all, the use of enameled metal tiles) adopted in residences and filtered through the complexity of a building that seeks the same excellent imprimatur of form, not only in the plan but also in the elevation. This is tangible in the concurrence of theoretical assumptions and potentiality, constructional yet also real, reconciled by the dynamic energy of these facilities denoted by extraordinary historical memories.

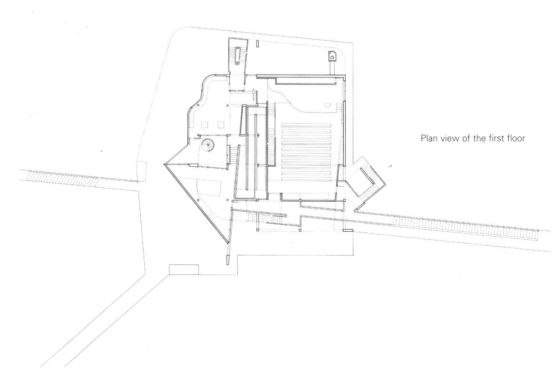

Plan view of the first floor

Section and view of the entrance façade

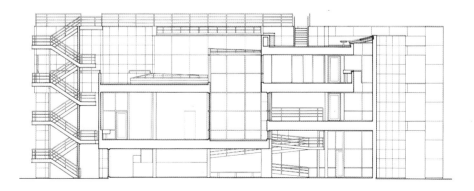

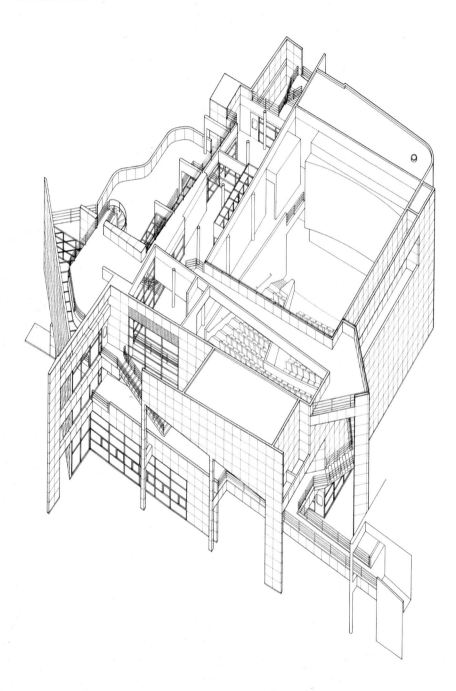

High Museum of Art
Atlanta, Georgia, 1980–83

A milestone in Meier's museum design repertoire, the High Museum is a veritable collage of many of the architect's building elements, expanded to this specific area.

In Atlanta, the complexities of the residential theme move into the public arena. In Atlanta, the planimetric system of lines of force is affirmed, as are the definitions of the functional and "utilization" systems. Atlanta is where the concept of exceptional memories is legitimized and re-elaborated. And where fine-tuned spatial sequences discover their natural confluence. In Atlanta Meier's odd non-monumental monumentality is born and affirmed, using volumes and masses that would later become less "volume" and "mass" and ever less defined. Atlanta marks the debut of the curved line in a design concept that, until then, had been composed of ninety-degree or colliding angles.

The High Museum does not have two clearly defined sectors like nearly all Meier's other projects. The actual exhibition sector plays on the geometric configuration of a quadrant set between two rectangles. But it is at this junction where a line of force extends from the visual focus point that several episodes unfold, such as the auditorium and service area, and the abstractly outlined space of fibrillation within *ratio* we often observe in non-residential plans (Barcelona, Melville, Getty Center). We also find the niche propelled onto the street, another recurrent first step in Meier's grammar.

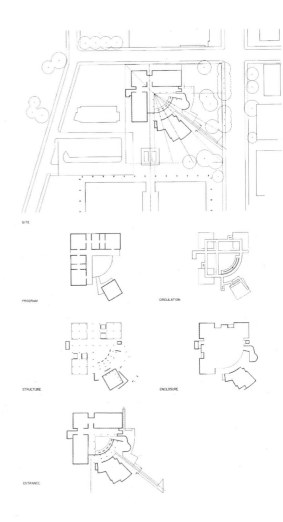

Relationship with the surroundings: site plan and analytical project diagrams

The museum viewed from the access ramp

Axonometric projection and
close-up of the exterior wall

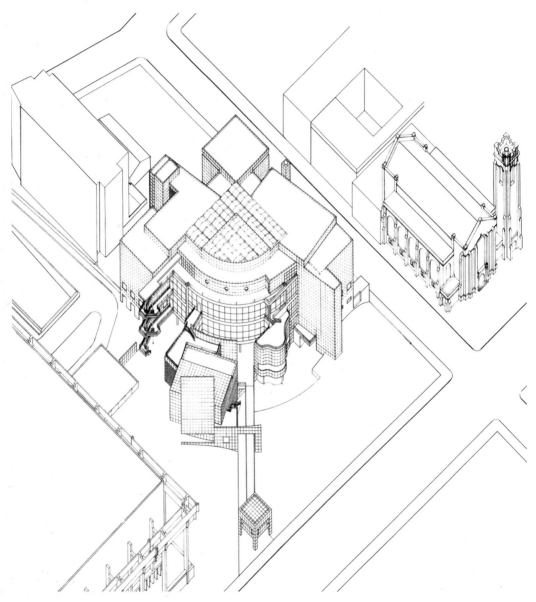

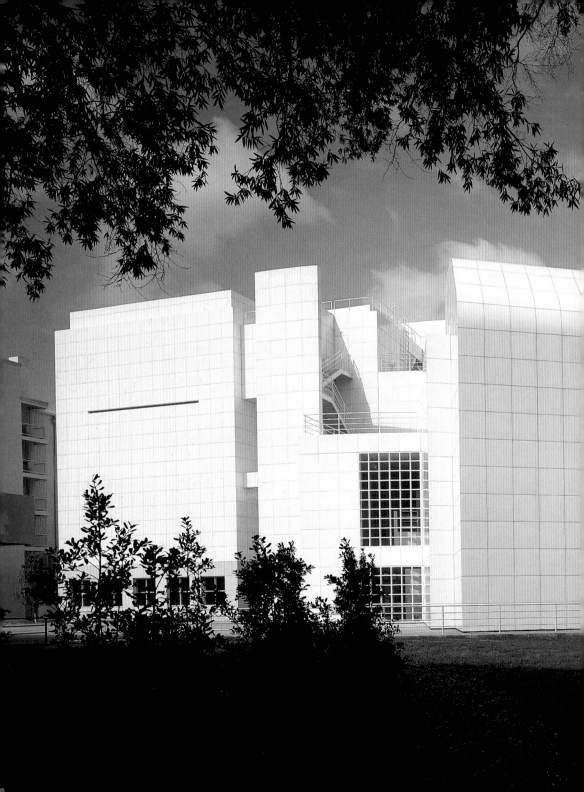

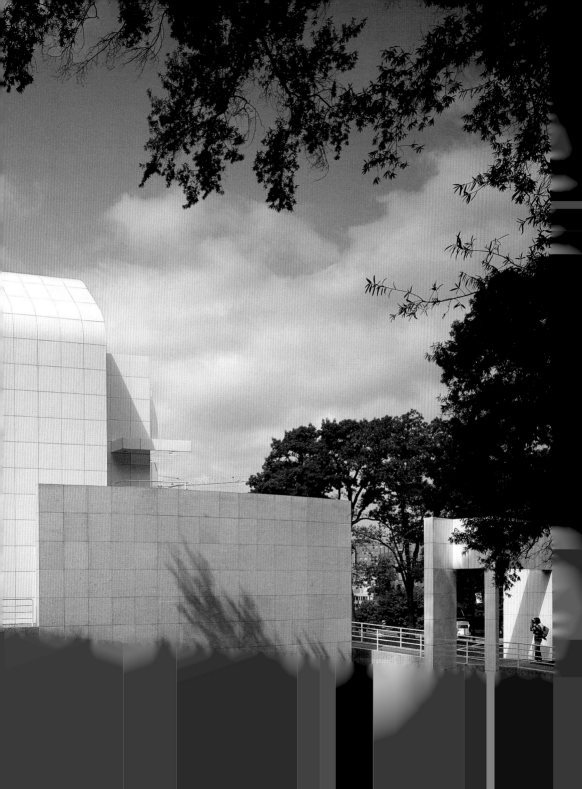

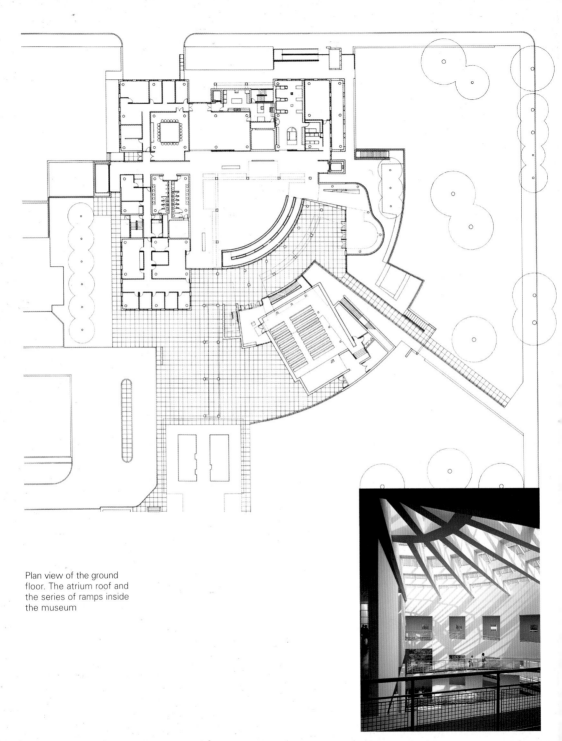

Plan view of the ground floor. The atrium roof and the series of ramps inside the museum

The Getty Center
Los Angeles, California, 1985–97

The theme is vast, ideal and uncommon: designing an art city in the Brentwood hillsides. Richard Meier strives for architectural diversification by blending allusions to the hill towns of central Italy with fragments of Villa Adriana, arranging the entire center on the rationality of two staggered grids that dominate the site's orographic complexity.

The program is equally complex and ambitious, with schools, workshops, museums and classrooms.

The solution involved isolating the complex from traffic by having visitors stop at the foot of the hill, at what is effectively a "landing place" with parking. A tram leaves this area to go to the Center, whose layout provides several focal points that act as visual landmarks, such as the auditorium and the Institute of the History of Art. These focal points are used as both compositional and scenic mainstays within an urban environment more concerned about its integration with the hilly terrain than about the buildings themselves. The completed project is the outcome of a series of adjustments and changes made over the years. Nonetheless, it mirrors the initial idea, though marred by several interventions such as the open-air amphitheater, which would have represented the proper conclusion of the compositional system set along the radians of the base grids. "No single space defines the Getty: it depends on your mood."

The Getty Center is essentially a sequence of spaces and courtyards: areas in which to ponder and observe places across and through this particular venue.

Enriched by a skillful balance of materials (mainly travertine and metal), Meier confronts the total design problem by diluting moments of abstraction and contextuality in favor of a composition that privileges urban planning. Thus, he leaves the power of the creative gesture inside *objets trouvés* with few parallels in contemporary architecture.

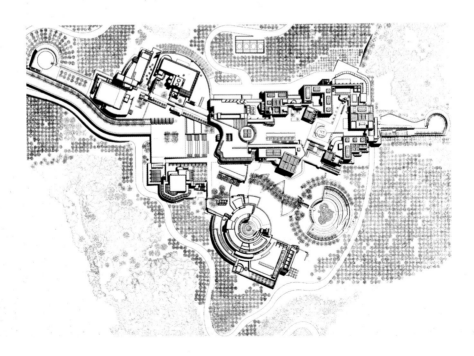

Volumetric plan and a view
of the museum courtyard

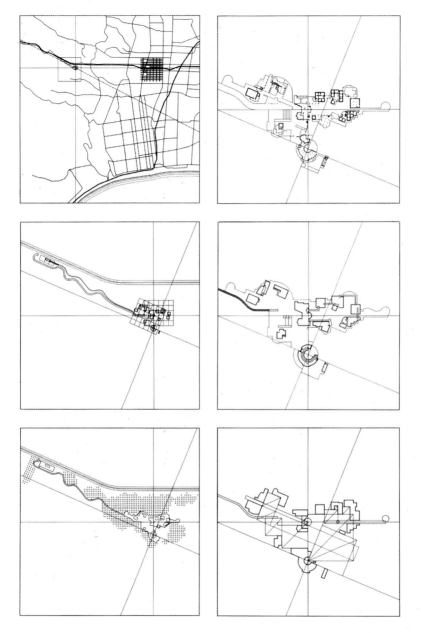

Analytical diagrams of the design versions:
surrounding area, structure, geometry, circulation, landscape, exterior space

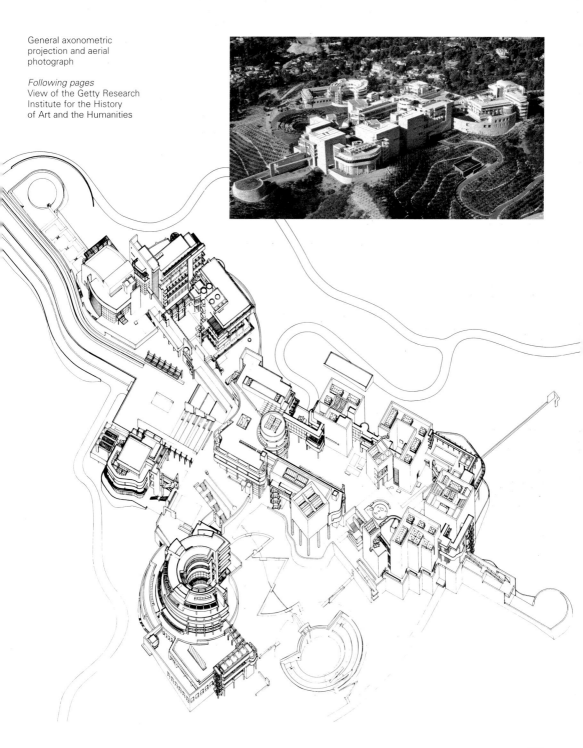

General axonometric
projection and aerial
photograph

Following pages
View of the Getty Research
Institute for the History
of Art and the Humanities

Plan views of the entrance
level and first floor

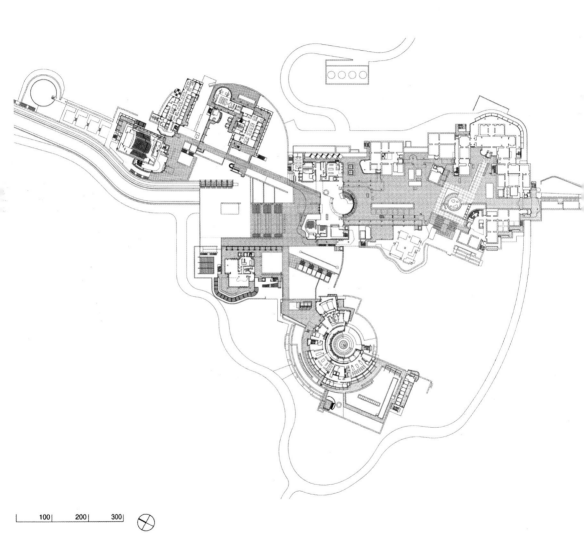

| 100| 200| 300|

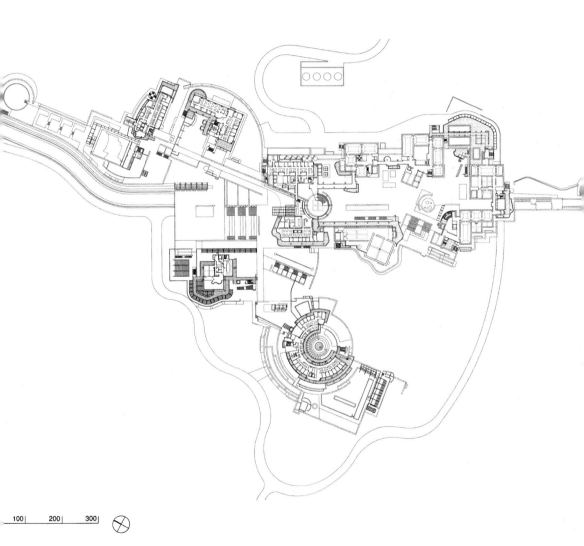

100| 200| 300|

41

The south entrance and
a close-up of the brise-soleil

Canal Plus Headquarters
Paris, France, 1988–92

The building housing the headquarters of the Canal Plus television station is the outcome of an international competition with a symbolic and representative intent.

The site is important because of its location along the river. The project thus follows the program and regulation guidelines, setting the complex in an L-shape along the perimeter of the assigned lot.

The complex has two main areas: an administrative wing that can clearly be discerned in the eight floors along the façade facing the Seine, and the squat sprawling production wing, separated from the administrative wing by the glazed entrance gallery. Two perpendicular lines, one parallel to the Seine rotated slightly, represent both the strategy and matrix of the distribution layout. Both emerge onto the roof with a different depth, not only to define the borders of a larger inner courtyard, but, above all – for the one skirting the river – to create a division between public and private.

This partition, which is thinner than envisaged in the original project, thus becomes a super-screen against with and with which to work using staggered floors. The result is a juxtaposition of full-empty, solid-transparent (witness how the curved glass wall is valorized). But it is also an arrangement that mediates the urban setting, as demonstrated by the large gash at the top, which underscores the intention of lightness and transparency characteristic of the entire project.

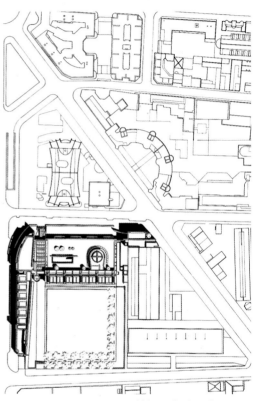

Volumetric plan, view of the corner layout and administrative wing

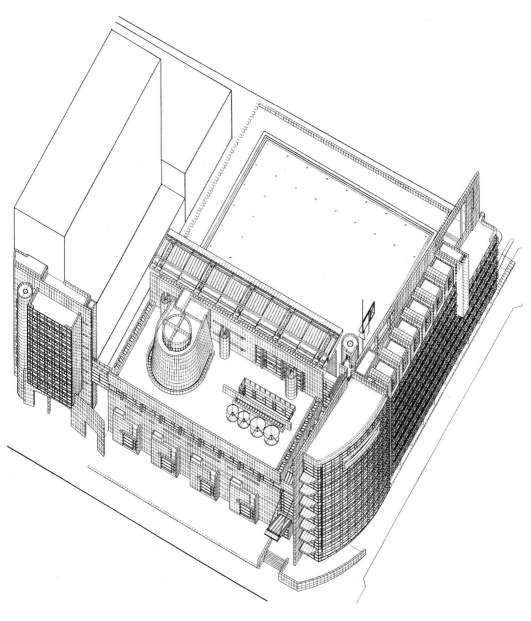

Plan view of the ground floor

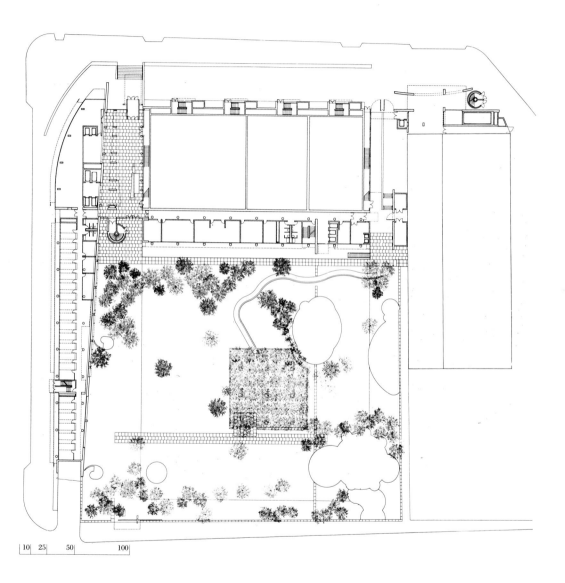

| 10 | 25 | 50 | | 100 |

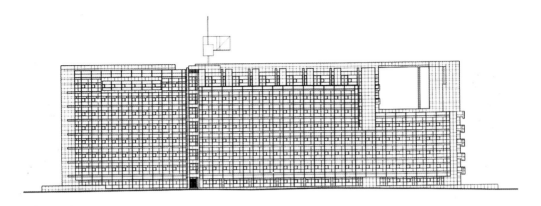

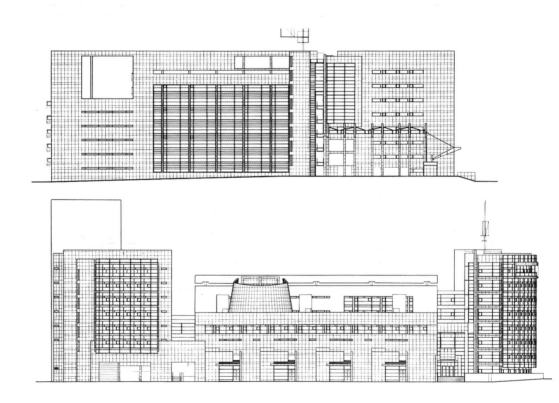

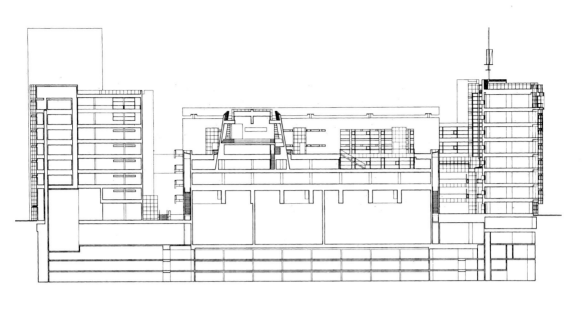

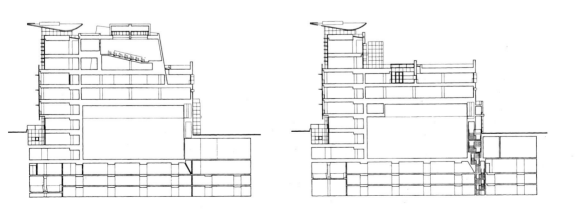

Close-ups of the corner
"hinge," at the internal
courtyard, and the
administrative wing

Museum of Contemporary Art
Barcelona, Spain, 1987–95

The Museum of Contemporary Art in Barcelona continues the architect's exploration of the rapport between ancient and modern. This study began in Ulm and continued with The Hague, Frankfurt, Munich and numerous projects completed to date in the heart of the Old World.

In Barcelona, Meier has created a precinct, a full-fledged plaza in the old quarters of the former convent of the Casa de la Caritat. By demolishing part of the urban fabric, he thereby recreates the layout of the museum complex.

The building complex also delineates another inner courtyard to the rear of the building. At this point, the project moves beyond the limitations of designing an individual unit and advances to reinterpret the extant. As for the interior layout, Meier has appropriated the circular ramps of Atlanta and straightened them, set against the transparent glass façade that is the true backbone of the routes emerging at the roof level. This enormous partition, virtually two-dimensional, underscores the architectural firm's beloved design strategy of plying the line-circle relationship in the plan view.

The interplay of powerful memories is unleashed in the elevations, trapping transparency between the two solids of the entrance systems and the fibrillating abstract, quasi-suspended volume under which visitors must pass in order to enjoy the *paseo* of the outside access ramp tangent to the building. Inside, the use of black for the flooring – the horizontal plane – augments the complexity of the structures, with the vertical planes orienting the visitors through natural lighting from the skylights and constructional intersections.

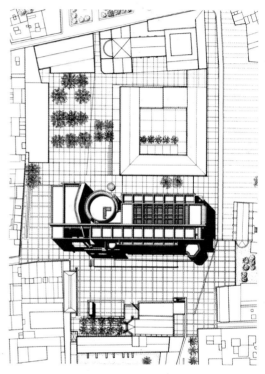

Area plan and view looking towards the entrance

The memories "grasped"
in the diagrams of the
overall compositional
strategy, and a view
of the plaza façade

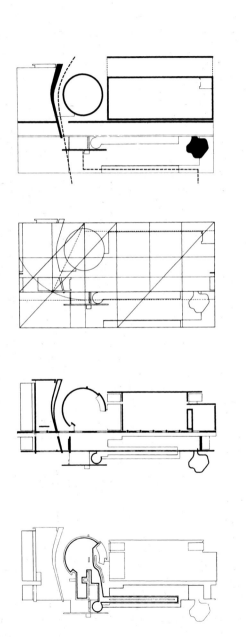
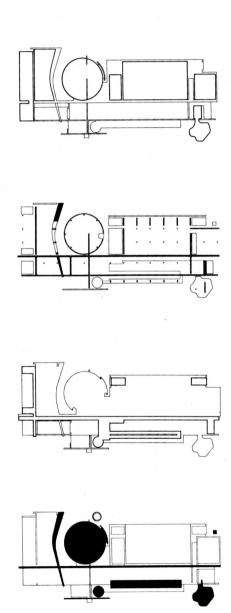

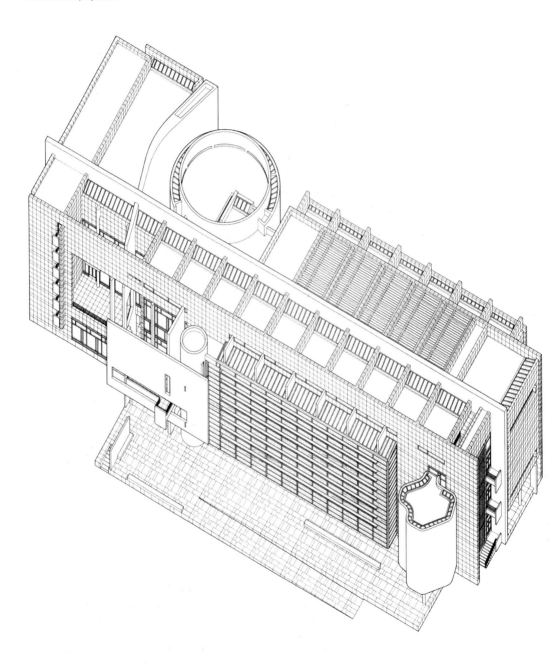

Plan views of the first floor and ground floor

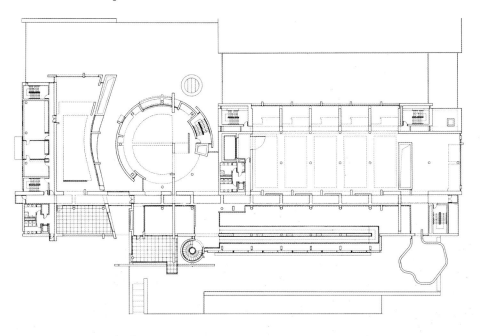

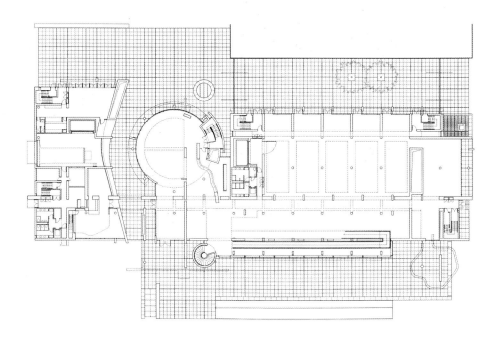

Façades of Plaça dels
Angels and of the internal
courtyard, and sections of
the entrance and exhibition
area

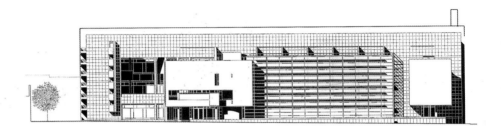

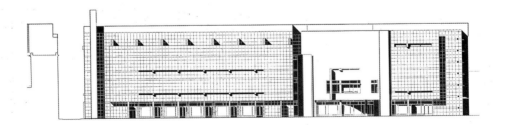

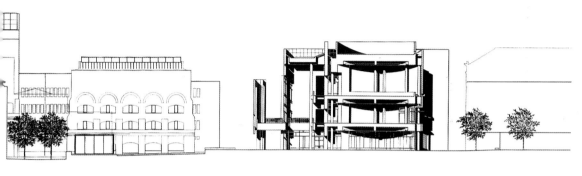

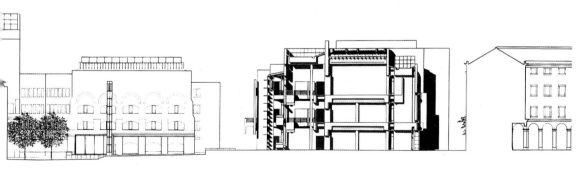

Swissair North American Headquarters
Melville, New York, 1991–94

The US headquarters of Swissair, the building in Melville, not far from New York City, limits itself to organizing the program, bringing out known allusions, and foreshadowing an interest in the concept of the glass curtain wall that would be accentuated in later works.

The project starts with a rectangular plan, thrust partially into the ground at the south façade. This façade is reminiscent of layouts that have already been used (Barcelona), but it clearly manifests the attempt at lightness in the sequence of staggered slabs clad with panels of enameled aluminum. Beyond this is a two-story hallway that runs along the entire length of the building.

The northern façade is intentionally simplified. Here, the viewer's attention is drawn to the detailing of the *brise-soleil* and the long glass façade, interrupted by the rising cylindrical volume (the meeting room), the service wall and the slab of the exterior staircase.

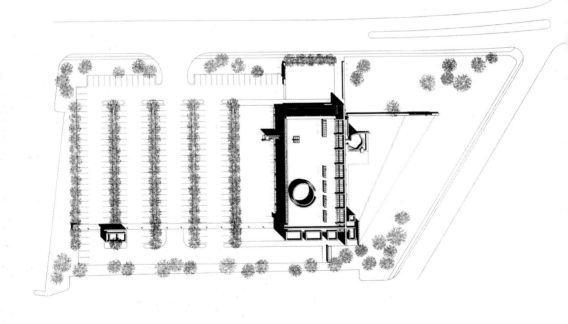

The building and site in the area plan

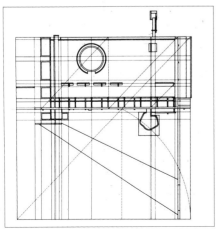

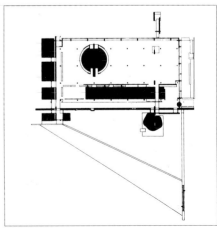

Spatial composition diagrams
and view of the north façade

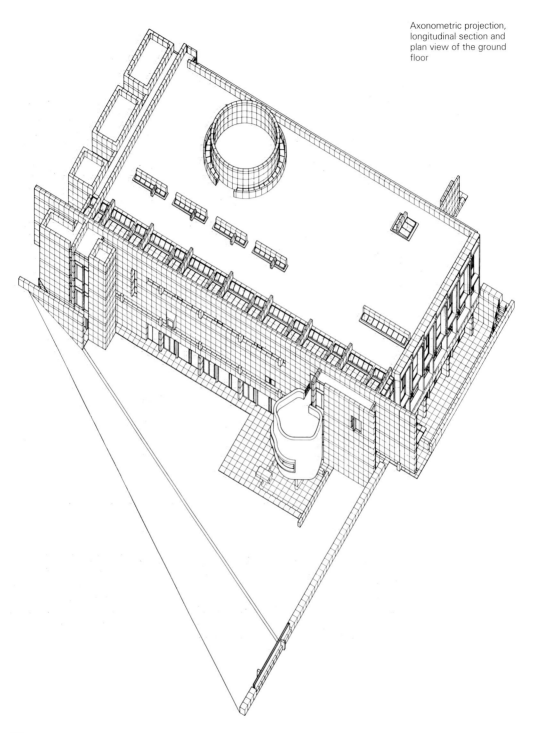

Axonometric projection, longitudinal section and plan view of the ground floor

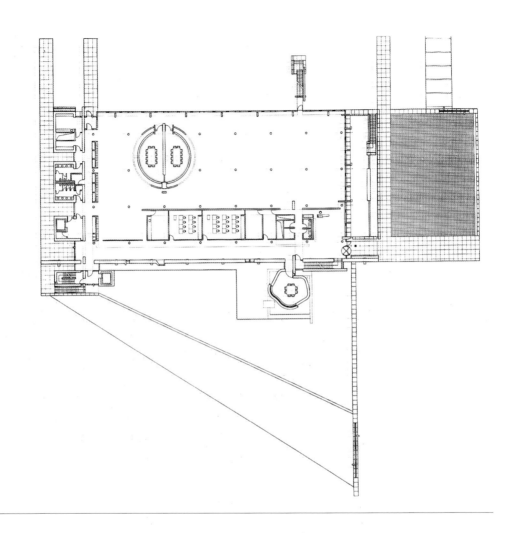

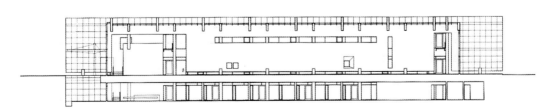

The east façade and the
internal gallery

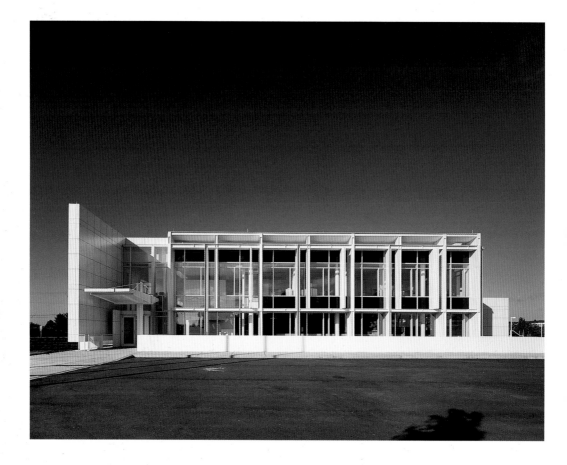

Rachofsky House
Dallas, Texas, 1991–96

The tactical systems used by Richard Meier often turn to analogous themes. The house theme is indubitably congenial to him. In one way or another, even after introducing the panel cladding system, his exploration of the possibilities expressed by ostensibly simple volumes harks back to basic geometries and to models that, likewise, are seemingly standard. Richard Meier's design concept is not merely formal invention without further explanation – though it is also that – but an exploitation of the infinite possibilities that geometric forms and almost-regular volumes can offer within a language whose parts have now become archetypes. These include the metal staircase abutting a slab, the cylindrical volumes, the partitions clad in sheet metal, and more. Meier works with the conviction that the relationships involved in constructing spaces encompass a balance of dialectics: simple and complex, transparent and solid. Thus, these elements are ascribable to a solution only if they are allowed to filter down through control over the technique that makes them possible, and this is not negated but incorporated into the entire process. Conflict must not be placated but merely made visible, accepting the unexpected.

The Rachofsky House is one of the many examples of the definition and indefinition of space. The plans are simple, the elevations are reduced to slabs, the volume is that of a parallelepiped, created and denied, to make spaces of exhibition – as is the case with all Meier's houses.

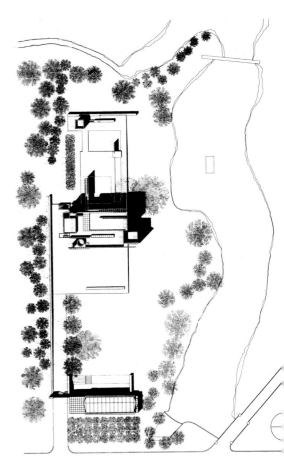

Area plan

Spatial composition
diagrams and view
of the west façade

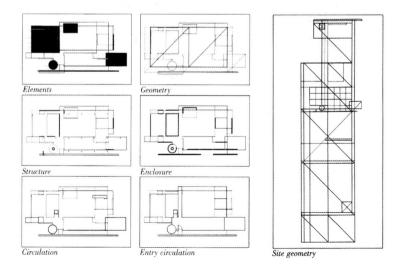

Elements

Geometry

Structure

Enclosure

Circulation

Entry circulation

Site geometry

Composition system in the
axonometric projection, and
a close-up of the east façade

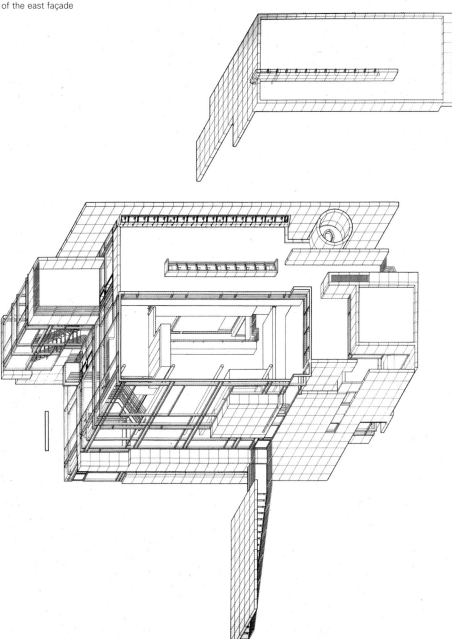

Plan view of the ground
floor, and the longitudinal
and transverse sections

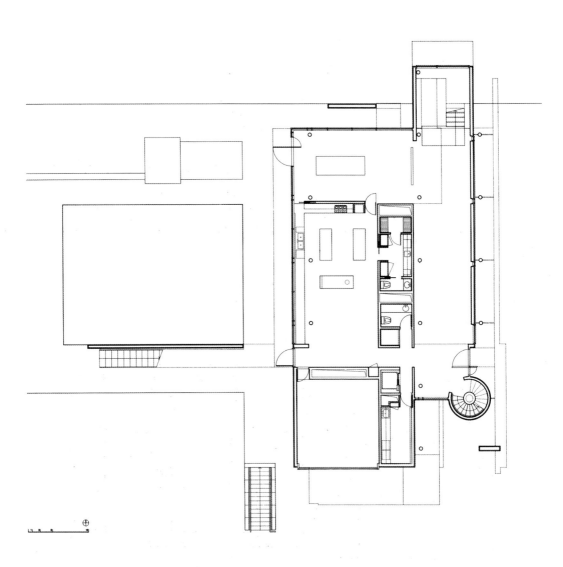

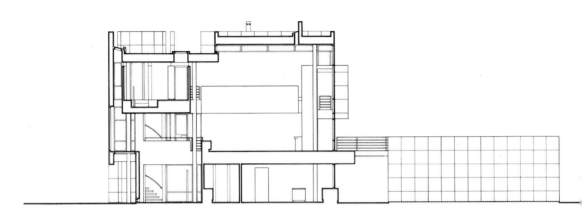

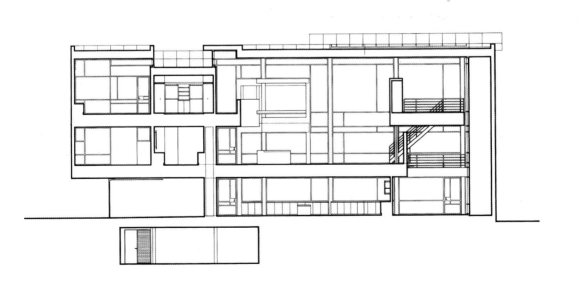

Islip Federal Courthouse
Islip, New York, 1993–2000

The Islip Federal Courthouse aspires to represent an effective urban pole by setting a hefty building along the highway that skirts the Atlantic on Long Island. Highly visible and imposing, the building manipulates the expression of its functions and of the image typical of federal buildings. It does this above all through the projection of a monumental, mysterious conical volume at the entrance. But it also achieves this through the chromatic contrast of stone against the pallor of the enormous framework, that shields the southeast façade. This is the farthest projecting façade, visible from the main thoroughfare.

Extraordinary diagrams illustrate Meier's customary compositional mechanisms. In the parabola of the *brise-soleil* – it does not adhere to the façade but is gently elliptical – several of the plans hold a similar allure, presaging fragments of the compositional criterion of the Jubilee Church. The project is influenced by the experience of the multipurpose buildings completed in The Hague, Munich and Paris. Indeed, traces can be found in the grandeur of the atrium which separates the two areas at the intersection with the axis of the frustum-shaped volume of the entrance. This acts as an axis and circulation space linking the courtrooms and offices.

The entire complex is set on a base outlining the area and containing its autonomy, creating the customary arrangement of accesses via ramps and stairs tangent to the exterior.

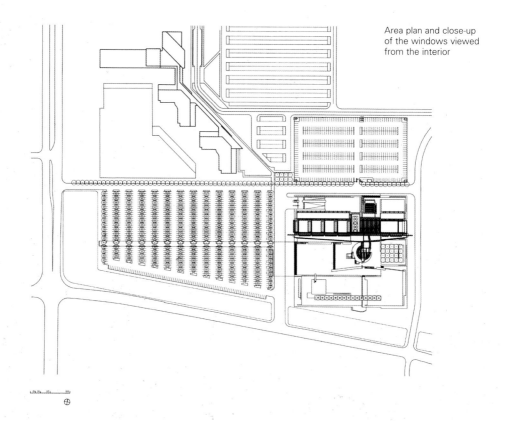

Area plan and close-up of the windows viewed from the interior

The entrance and the
southwest façade

Straight line-circumference
and cylinder-parallelepiped
studies in the analytical
and spatial composition
diagrams

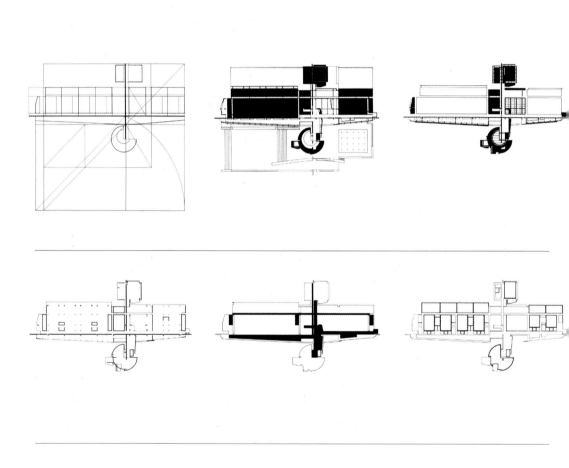

Plan view of the ground floor

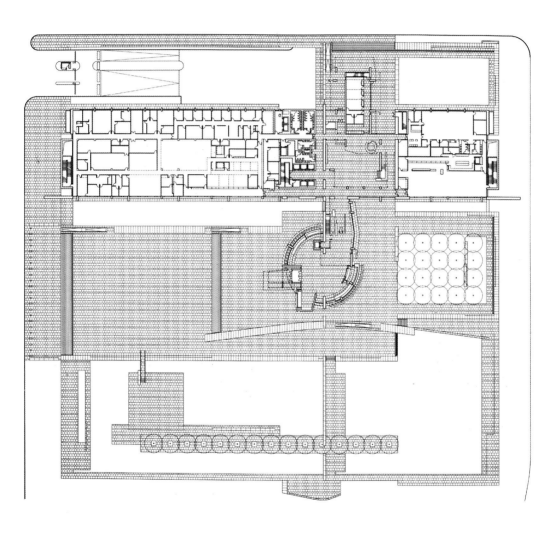

Transverse sections, and
close-ups of the entrance
overhang and one of the
rooms

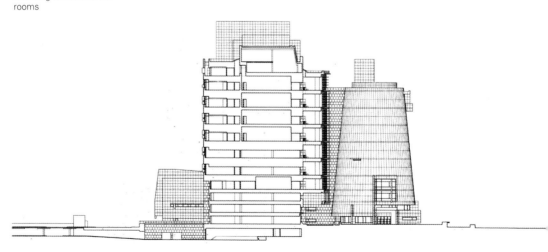

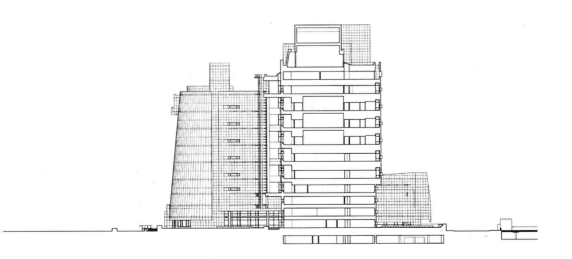

Neugebauer House
Naples, Florida, 1995–98

Straight line, circumference, podium: the Neugebauer House expands on the solid tradition of American Minimalism.

Just as the Farnsworth House lends drama to the Illinois countryside and the Kaufman House underscores the sheer power of the desert, this residence reaches out to the very edge of the sea, encompassing the ripple of the sandy shore in its design. Everything thus becomes perfectly artificial, indeed, naturally artificial – or vice-versa. In the calm drama of this temple-house, the cantilevered roof stigmatizes the terms of dimensions and turns every action into ritual: parking inside a squat cylindrical volume (the circle); pausing on the podium facing the sea; finding shelter in the shade of technology (again, the roof) that turns the hut into metaphor. The latter thus becomes a composition *en longueur*. Without any particular formal organization, it is merely a long sequence of distances and a single ambience. Estranged and extraneous, yet also ancient, the Neugebauer House is indubitably a moment of suspended equilibrium – an allusion to Magritte – in the struggle to dominate the fourth dimension, above and beyond the sense of function.

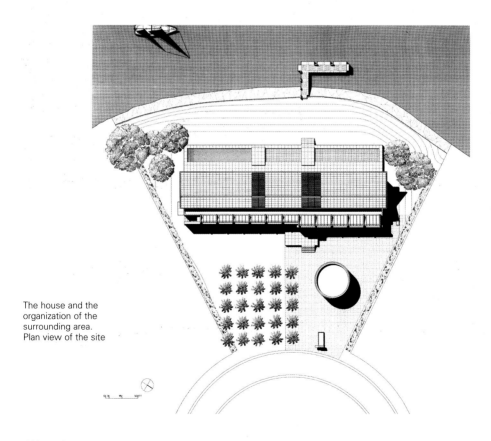

The house and the organization of the surrounding area. Plan view of the site

Section and view of the
façade towards the sea
from the west

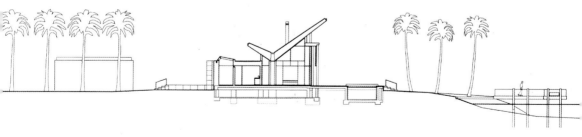

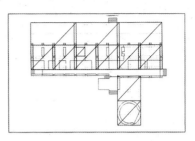
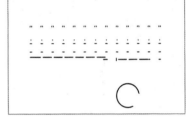
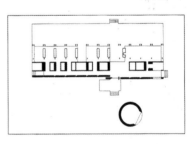
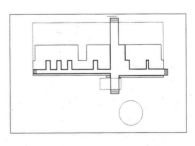

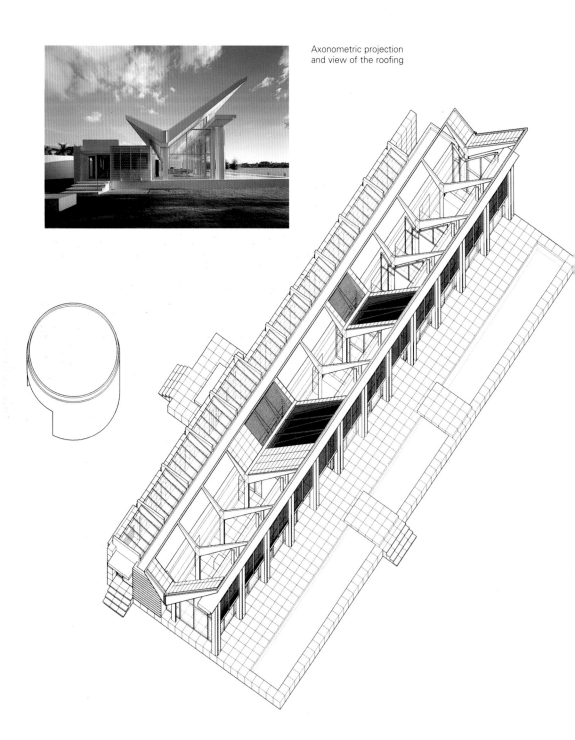

Axonometric projection
and view of the roofing

Plan view of the ground floor

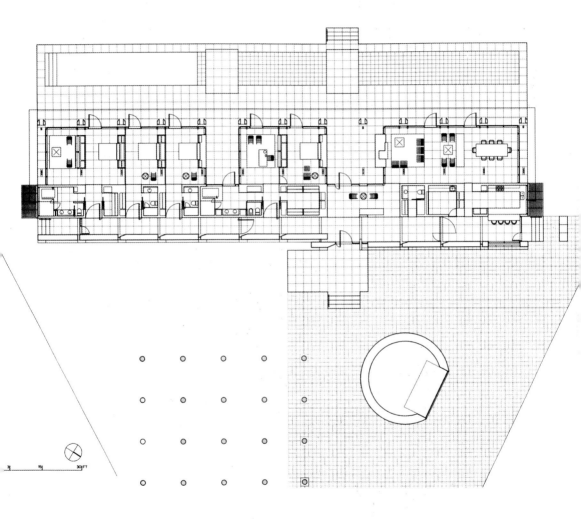

Jubilee Church
Rome, Italy, 1996–2003

The outcome of an international competition, the Jubilee Church at Tor Tre Teste confirms Meier's proclivity for using geometry as his compositional passkey in highly complex urban locations. Thus, he has attuned the autonomy of the designed object – in this case, the church-object – to this role but also in relation to the exterior, its surroundings.

The project is composed of two specific functional areas. One is devoted to the actual liturgical space, and the other to the parochial areas and functions (playing field, etc.).

The two situations are perfectly visible in the plan, which unhinges the orthogonal arrangement of the generating "geometries," and in the elevation, which shows the contrast of the curve and the straight line. But the intent of this *recherche* is to mingle – in a single, sculptural setting – the sensuality of the enormous shells with the relative rigidity of the areas not strictly liturgical. Barely touching the ground and powerfully carved on the inside, these shells of pigmented reinforced concrete do not seem to overlap. Instead, they expand in an attempt to create a nonexistent center in the area and define a space that is enclosed yet filtered. This strategy avoids transparencies, which converge at the roof – glazed and effectively nonexistent.

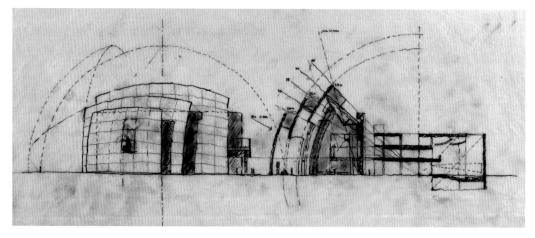

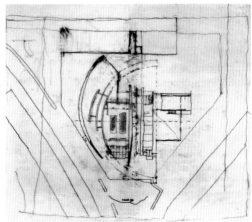

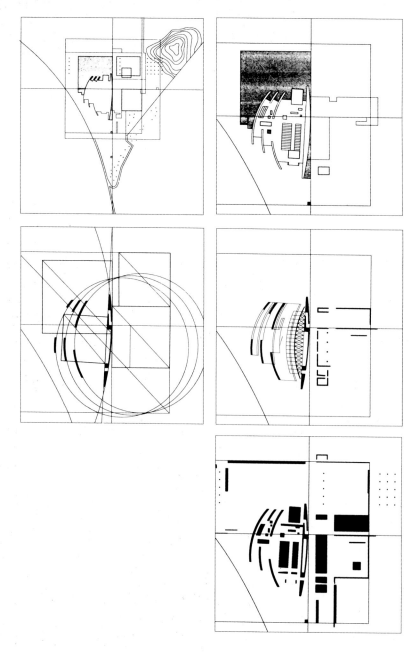

Plan view of the site
and the entrance façade

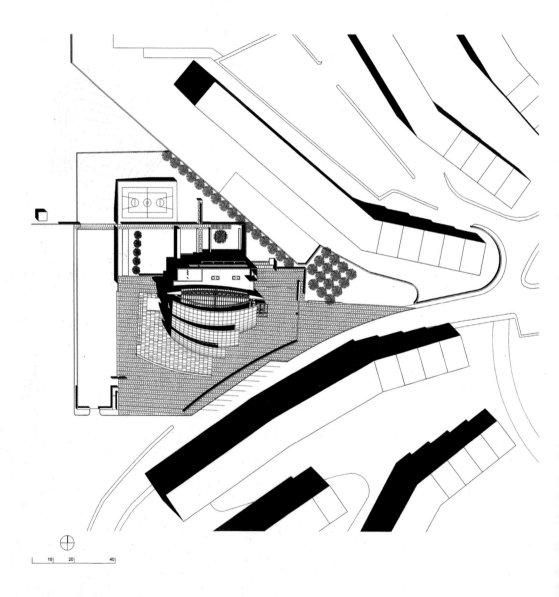

10 20 40

Plan view of the ground
floor, and the east and
west elevations

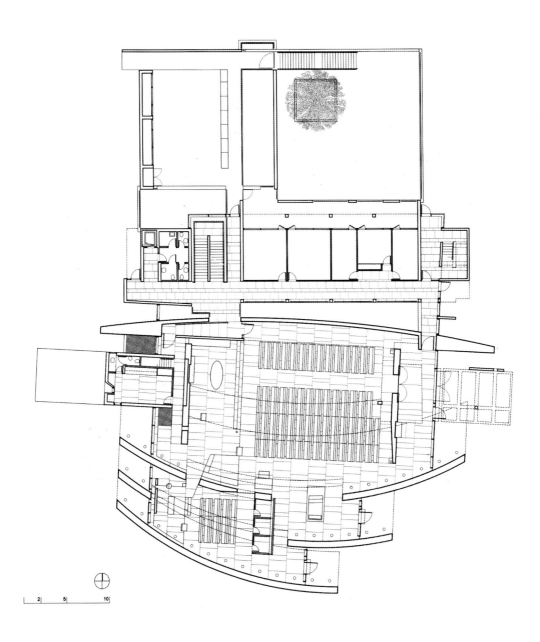

2 5 10

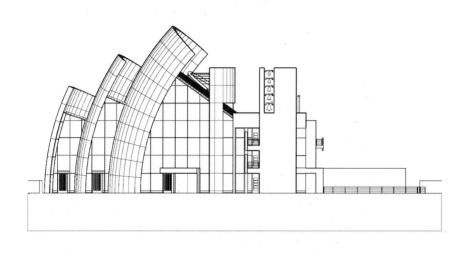

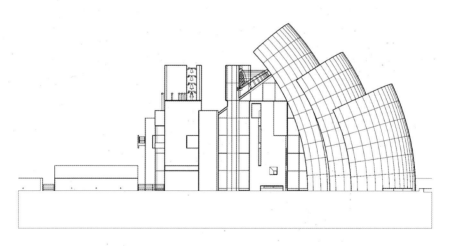

The east and west façades,
and two longitudinal
sections

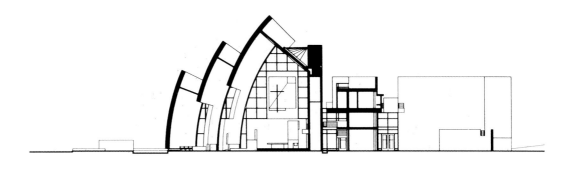

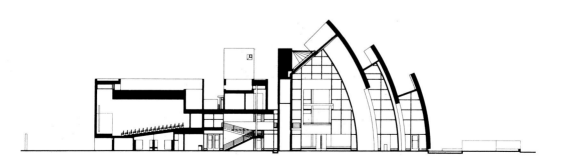

The parochial areas, the "shells" of the south façade, and two transverse sections

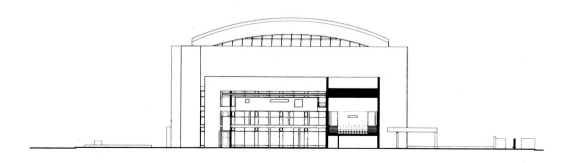

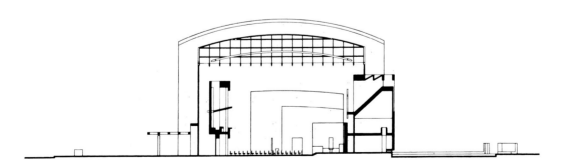

Ara Pacis Museum
Rome, Italy, 1996

This difficult and controversial project in the heart of a key area in Western history involved Augustus' Ara Pacis, a major religious monument of ancient Rome, dating back to the ninth century B.C. The project entailed intervening in the area Vittorio Morpurgo earmarked in 1937, once the excavation work was completed under the foundations of Palazzo di Fiano near the Tiber. Aside from the objective difficulties inherent in both theme and place, the project also required space for a small museum, a small auditorium and annexed services.

It is clear that the project cannot be grouped among those of simple museums, due to its historic stratifications and symbolism as well as the narrow intervention margins and restricted space. Above all, however, it had to deal with the difficulties inherent in a direct parallel between contemporary and ancient architecture, experienced here without any mediation.

Meier sited the project in the area tangent to the street and the Lungotevere or riverfront, positioning it on two floors. The ground floor, naturally favored as the exhibition base, is set between the wall, glass and another wall, as a way of downplaying the solemnity of an enclosure striving to be just that, rather than architecture per se.

Purified of all connotative aspects, the project seems to focus on identifying a volume that is subdued and intricate yet vital in relation to extremely historicized perspectives or visual cues – the surroundings, the river, immediate existences – avoiding any reinterpretation of the significance of memory.

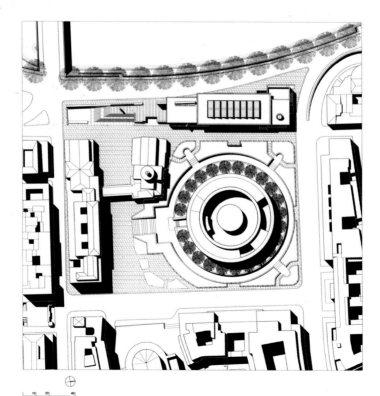

10| 20| 40|

Plan view of the site, west
façade and simulated view
from the Tiber riverfront

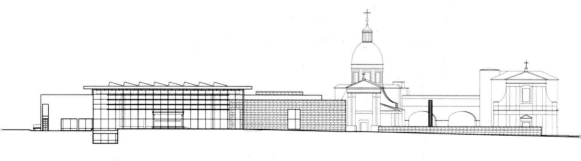

Plan view of the ground
floor, section and
photographs of the
building site

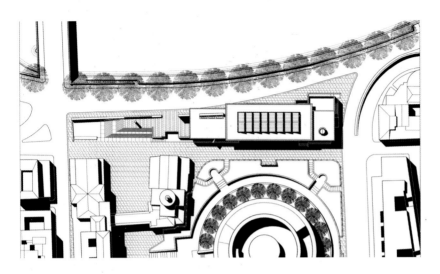

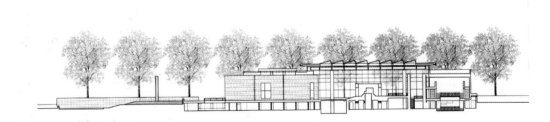

Visitor Center of the Crystal Cathedral
Orange Grove, California, 1996

The Visitor Center of the Crystal Cathedral in Orange Grove reworks a theme typical of Meier's repertoire. The rapport between the sphere (cylinder) and the straight line (parallelepiped) has manifested moments of absolute complementariness, most clearly in the residential sector.

Like the Atheneum, this project involved preparing a space essentially outfitted for thorough utilization. At Orange Grove two straight lines – one tangent to the plan sphere and the other secant to it – define a geometric genesis that is lost in the elevations, where the cylinder fades into the sequence of enveloping partitions, fire escapes and volumes implanted in the kaleidoscope of internal space. It is perceived in the elevations as a sequence of enclosing elements.

Area plan

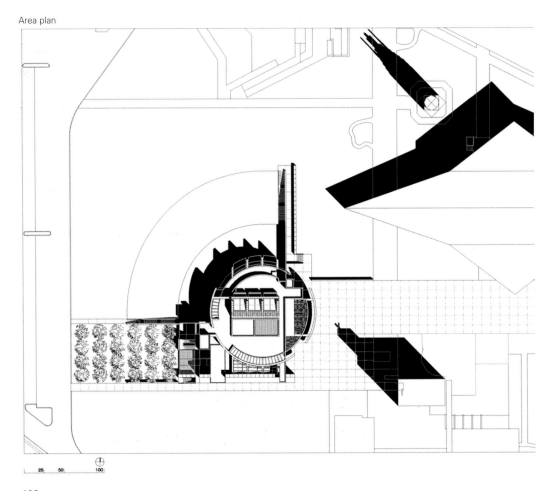

| 25 | 50 | | 100 |

East façade and insertion
of the model in the area.
Philip Johnson's Crystal
Cathedral is visible on the
right

Plan views of the ground
floor and first floor, and
the south, west and north
elevations

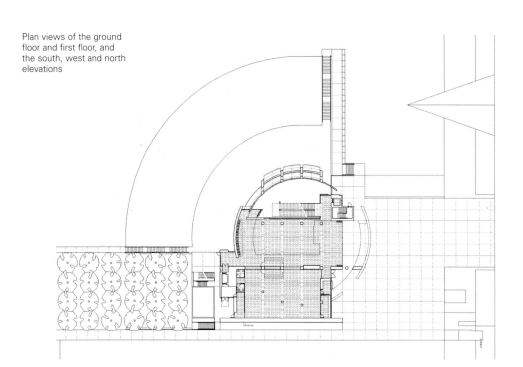

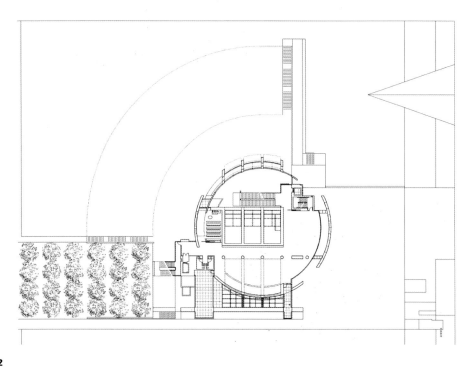

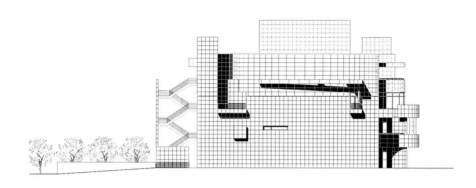

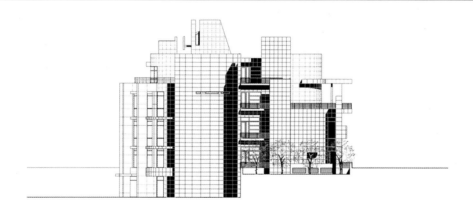

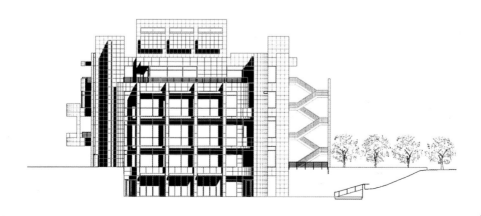

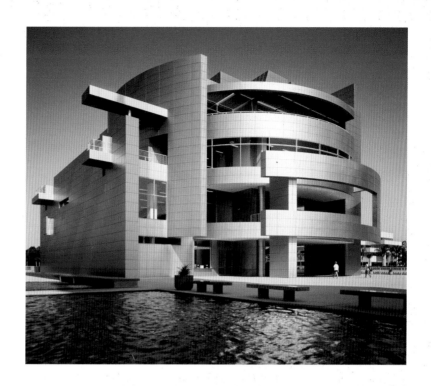

Rickmers Reederei Center
Hamburg, Germany, 1998-2001

By playing precisely on the intrinsic qualities of facework, the Rickmers Reederei Center continues the process of dematerializing constructed works, undertaken years ago and examined in greater depth during the Nineties. The project is modest as far as size is concerned, with three floors and a basement level near other buildings and a lake. And yet its outcome is utterly unique.

At the Rickmers, the fragmentation of the volumetric system of the parallelepiped reveals forms of freedom and conclusions that are "unexpected" for those who see only the simplicity of the plans, which are rather "orthodox" in their overall distribution. They are unexpected because of the disappearance of white,

overwhelmed by the transparency and opacity of glass preponderant here, and the intentional absence of the materiality typical of enameled metal tiles.

These tiles retain eclectically assembled shards that stir Dutch and constructivist memories. This allusion is also achieved through the determined intrusion of the verticality of the windows in the staggered interplay of the overlapping structures (the bearing structures and the glass ones), as well as the projecting floor slabs used to create balconies and terraces. This reveals an arrangement of floors interlocking both horizontally and vertically – a concept unexplored by Meier's language until then.

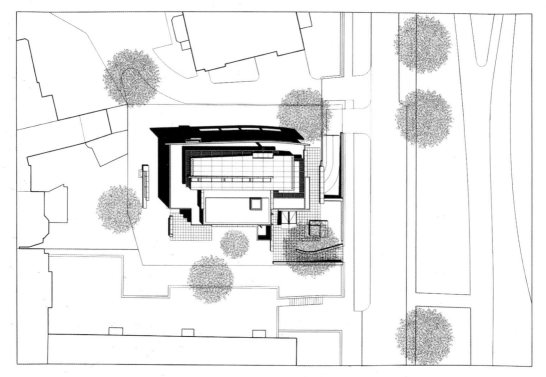

Area plan and the east façade

Two views of the southeast façade

Plan view of the ground floor,
section at the entrance,
and close-up of the corner
of the north façade

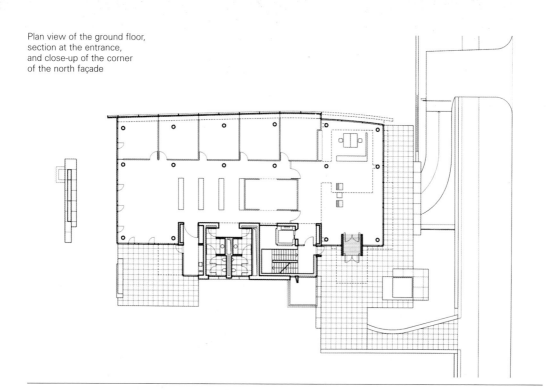

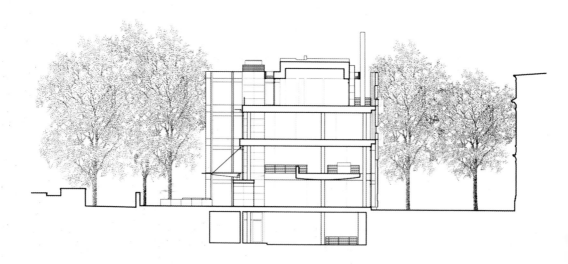

East façade and terrace

Project for the bridge at Cittadella
Alessandria, Italy, 1998–2006

The project for the bridge at Cittadella reveals an unusual Meier, tackling the kind of structuralism that can be glimpsed in the roofing at Bethel (NY 2001). Here, however, the spatial implications are more evident and enthralling with respect to the function inherent in the very nature of a bridge. The formal exemplification that is pursued is nevertheless evident. The enormous parabola is given the task of acting as the main bearing structure. As a result, the horizontal element it supports does not merely act as a mediator but, in the analogy of form, it effectively acquires its own spatial definition.

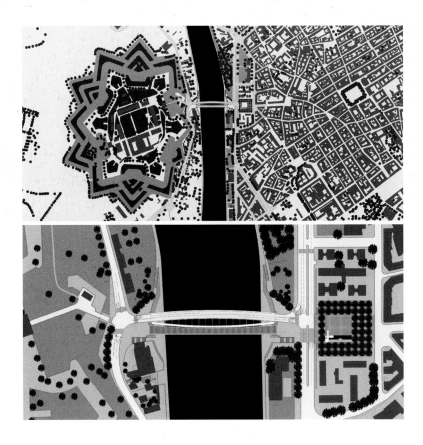

173-176 Perry Street
New York, New York, 1999–2002

Overlooking the Hudson River at the edge of the yet-untouched Tribeca area, these two buildings – virtually twins – tackle the theme of transparency in New York's medium-height residential buildings. They are not true towers, yet they are not condominiums either.

Currently widespread – in terms of size – in the areas being eroded by new construction in Manhattan, which is undergoing constant transformation often at the expense of the classic "low" brick residential fabric, this pseudo-condominium type has recently become a cliché, particularly uptown. Traces of this are evident at Perry Street solely in the use of the balcony, an element that has now come into vogue in North America. Here, it is incorporated into the overall volume and is used purely compositionally. Though similar, the façades differ in several ways, striving to eliminate the corporeal aspect of the cladding, reduced here to a "screen." The rotation and rhythm of the elements,

which are always the same, on the various façades reiterate the sense of privacy and the residential function of the buildings. Richard Meier's plans follow the outline of the street fronts, only pushing back the façades on Perry Street. As a result, in addition to creating a small internal plaza on the entrance side, he also distances and highlights the façades on the West Side Highway.

The layouts are almost identical; there are only two apartment types: one or two bedrooms, and they stand out from the bordering buildings through the projection of the stairwell-elevator shaft and the living-room areas on the façade facing the river. The project emphasizes the potential of intervening in highly distinctive urban areas by developing a language that, albeit sophisticated, does not merge with the rigid expressive vocabulary so strongly linked to the architecture of the service industry.

Elevations on the
Hudson River, and view
of the towers from
New Jersey

Plan views of the floors for the one- and two-bedroom apartments

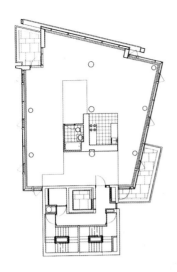

Frieder Burda Museum
Baden-Baden, Germany, 2001–04

The architect we observe at the Burda Museum is utterly orthodox and composed.

The problem here is akin to the one at the Frankfurt Museum, probably the most successful of Richard Meier's "contextual" projects, in terms of dissonances, assonances, diversification, materials. At Frankfurt, however, the extant building exerts even greater pressure.

Baden-Baden involves proximity rather than coexistence, and the problem of comparisons and relations is attenuated. This link is entrusted to mild contamination: a simple, transparent and anonymous walk-way. What remains in both projects is the rigor of the composition and of the façades.

Almost all the façades are similar to those of the existing building, however, the ones on Richard Meier's building are alternative and rigorous.

With a square plan, an internal ramp that is not tangential to the façade framing two galleries – the main one covering just two levels – and the absence of intrusion or geometric contamination, the Frieder Burda Museum thus confirms its role as a poised, tranquil exercise of sublime composition.

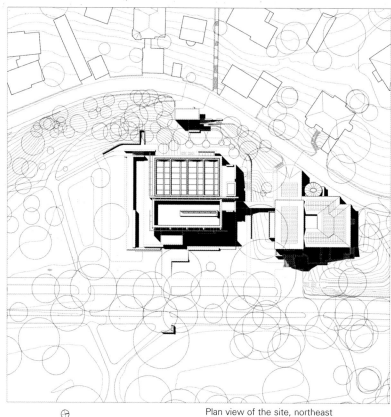

10 20

Plan view of the site, northeast
elevation, and model

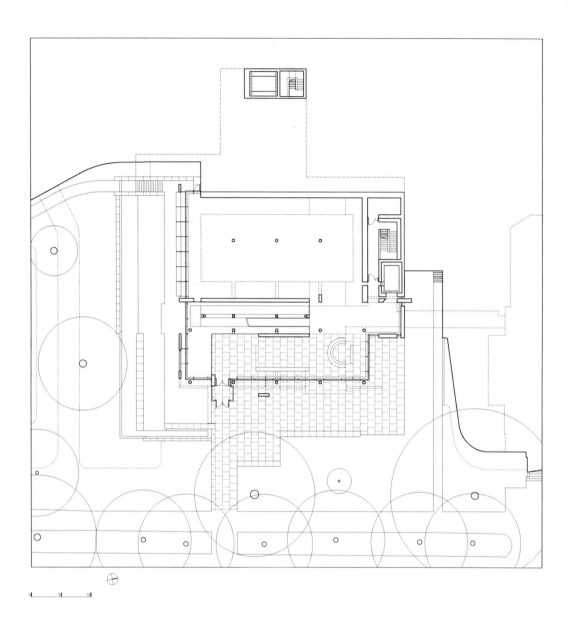

Plan views of the ground
floor and first floor

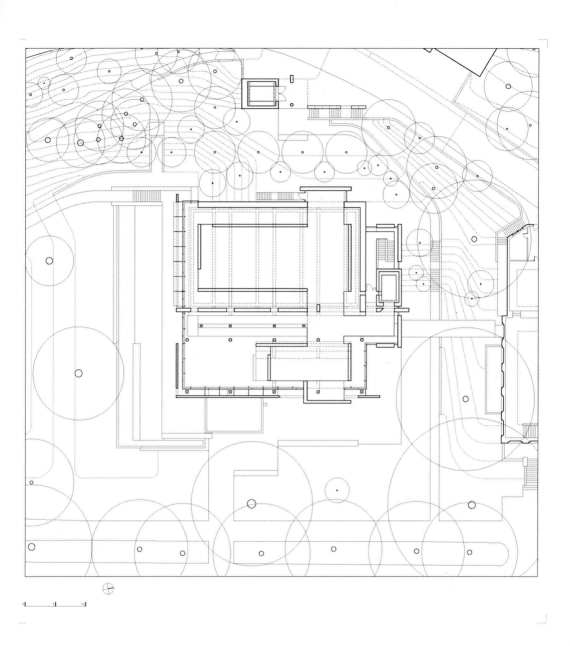

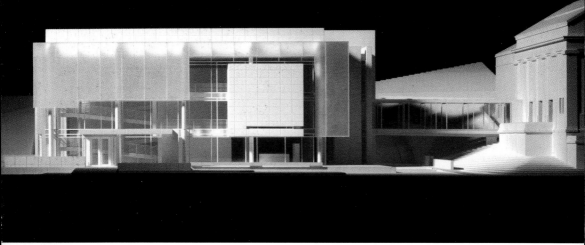

The building project, the
existing structures, and
sections through the ramp
and main gallery

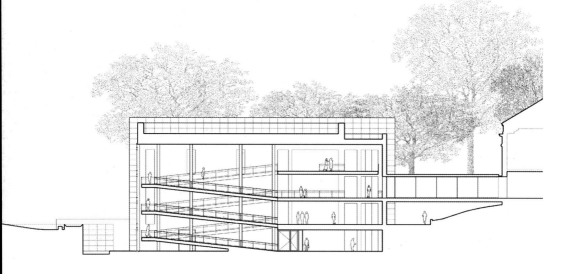

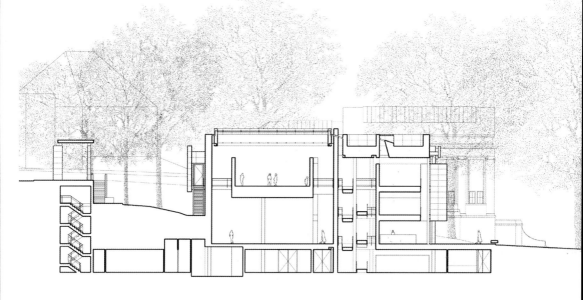

World Trade Center Proposal
New York, New York, 2001

Eisenman Architects,
Gwathmey / Siegel Associates
and Steven Holl Architects

Halted at the proposal stage together with the other projects shown to the general public, industry critics and others, the proposal for the World Trade Center remains one of the first true demanding confrontations with the American fabric since the days of the Chicago Tribune. For the architectural firm, it is a test played out on the New York game board, following on the heels of the exercise of the towers (two here as well) designed for the area of Madison Square Garden to the north.

Tackled as a group, the skyscraper theme successfully amalgamates the complexity of professional experience and superimposed ideals. It thus yields a concept with vast urban ramifications, concerned with identifying a solution that is not "specific" or overpoweringly individual.

The "enclosure" of an out-of-scale grid enveloping the north and west corners of the area is highly ambitious. Nonetheless, this is the very reason it is worthy of consideration, because it alters and calls into question the terms of the demands here, without entrusting them to the ennui of technology and gratuitous invention.

It is the urban precinct of a now-sacred area that leaves to memory the perimeter of the two towers, transformed into pools capable of "remembering" without rhetoric. *Ratio* is thus the predominant element of the composition, allowing itself to yield to exception, creative imagination included.

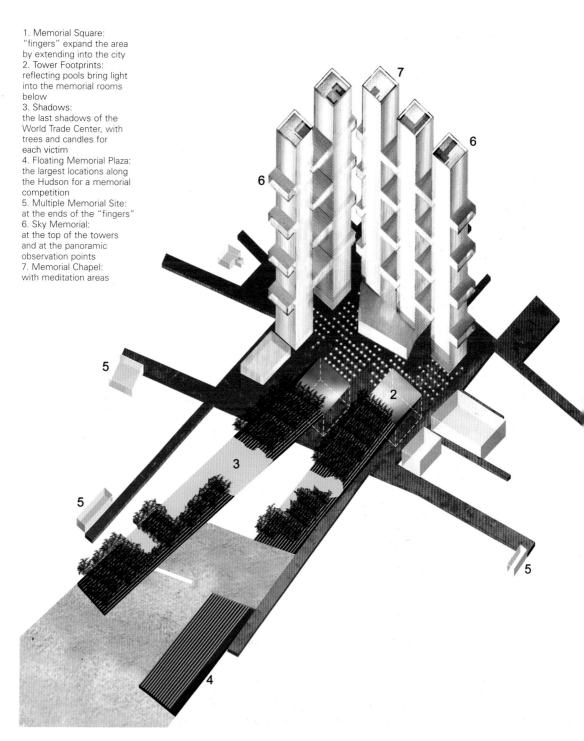

1. Memorial Square:
"fingers" expand the area
by extending into the city
2. Tower Footprints:
reflecting pools bring light
into the memorial rooms
below
3. Shadows:
the last shadows of the
World Trade Center, with
trees and candles for
each victim
4. Floating Memorial Plaza:
the largest locations along
the Hudson for a memorial
competition
5. Multiple Memorial Site:
at the ends of the "fingers"
6. Sky Memorial:
at the top of the towers
and at the panoramic
observation points
7. Memorial Chapel:
with meditation areas

Restaurant 66

New York, New York, 2002–03

Restaurant 66 is located at the corner of Church and Leonard, on the ground floor of the Textile Building designed by Henry Hardenbergh (Dakota Building, Plaza Hotel) in the early twentieth century. Richard Meier has stepped in here discreetly, but very decisively from an ideological standpoint, turning the place into a manifesto of the value and sense of "surface" interventions on exceptional extant structures.

The project tends to emphasize the power of the existing space and structures rather than overturning them. There is just one gesture: the semicircular and translucent element that separates the entrance from the series of fluid yet different spaces open to the public.

The rest is entrusted to the interaction of absolute colors, banners included, and to the uniformity of the cement floor platform used to hold and distinguish materials and colors, including the glass of some of the tables, the seating, and the Spartan faux neutrality of the chairs in gray metal mesh.

The semicircular volume of the atrium, views of the restaurant and its entrance

Appendix

Biography

Richard Meier studied architecture at Cornell University, and opened his studio in New York in 1963. He has been awarded major commissions for public buildings such as courthouses and city halls, and for museums, corporate headquarters, housing and private residences in the United States and Europe. Some of his best-known projects include the Getty Center in Los Angeles, the High Museum in Atlanta, Georgia, the Museum for Decorative Arts in Frankfurt, and the Barcelona Museum of Contemporary Art. In 1984, Meier was awarded the Pritzker Prize, the most important award in the field of architecture. In the same year, he was selected for the prestigious commission to design the new Getty Center in Los Angeles, which was inaugurated in December 1997. Enormously successful with the general public, the Getty Center also garnered great critical acclaim. Recent projects completed by the firm of Richard Meier & Partners include the towers at 173-176 Perry Street in New York, and the federal courthouses in Islip, New York, and Phoenix, Arizona. Meier's firm is also executing the Burda Collection Museum in Baden-Baden and the UCLA Broad Art Center in California. The firm is currently designing the Yale University History of Art and Arts Library, and the Cornell Life Sciences Technology Building in Ithaca, New York.

In 1997, Meier received the AIA Gold Medal, the most important award of the American Institute of Architects, and in the same year the Japanese government awarded him the Praemium Imperiale, in recognition of a lifetime achievement in the arts. He is a Fellow of the American Institute of Architects, receiving the Medal of Honor from the New York Chapter in 1980 and the Gold Medal from the Los Angeles Chapter in 1998. His numerous design awards include 29 National AIA Honor Awards and 51 New York AIA Design Awards. In 1989, the Royal Institute of British Architects (RIBA) awarded him the Royal Gold Medal. In 1992 the French government honored Meier as Commander of Arts and Letters, and in 1995 he was elected Fellow to the American Academy of Arts and Sciences. Meier has also been awarded honorary degrees from the University of Naples, the New Jersey Institute of Technology, the New School for Social Research of the Pratt Institute, and the University of Bucharest.

Bibliography

Five Architects: Eisenman, Graves, Gwathmey, Hejduk, Meier, Wittenborn, New York 1972 (Introductions by K. Frampton and C. Rowe).

R. Meier, *Architect: Buildings and Projects 1966-1976*, Oxford University Press, New York 1976 (Introduction by K. Frampton, Afterword by J. Hejduk).

G. Vigtel, R. Meier, A. Anthony, *High Museum of Art – The New Building: A Chronicle of Planning, Design and Construction*, High Museum of Art, Atlanta 1983.

Richard Meier Architect, Rizzoli, New York 1984 (Preface by R. Meier, Introduction by J. Rykwert, Afterword by J. Hejduk).

Progetto Bicocca, Electa, Milan 1986.

V. Vaudou, editor, *Richard Meier/Monographies*, Electa, Milan 1986 (R. Meier, *Avant-propos*; H. Damisch, *La Modernité comme seuil*; H. Ciriani, *Radieuse modernité*; D. Lewis, *Sur Richard Meier*; J. Mas, *La capture du regard*).

W. Blaser, *Richard Meier: Building for Art*, Birkhäuser Verlag, Basel 1990.

R. Meier, *Architecture/Projects 1986-1990*, Centro Di Florence 1991.

V. Magnago Lampugnani, *Museums Architektur in Frankfurt 1980-1990*, Prestel-Verlag, Munich 1990 (D. Bartetzko, *Unity in Diversity*; K. Frampton, *Magnificent Chaos*).

L. Nesbitt, *Richard Meier: Collages*, St. Martin's Press, New York 1990 (*The Art of Abstraction*, interview of Richard Meier by Clare Farrow).

A.C. Papadakis, editor, *The New Modern Aesthetic*, Art and Design, Great Britain 1990 (K. Frampton, *Richard Meier and the City in Miniature*; R. Meier, C. Jencks, D. Libeskind and C. Jameson, *The Tate Gallery Discussion*; transcription of R. Meier's conference *The Annual Architecture Forum*).

Richard Meier, Academy Editions, Great Britain 1990 (K. Frampton, *Richard Meier and the City in Miniature*; C. Jencks, *Richard Meier Interviews 1980-1988*; R. Meier, *RIBA Royal Gold Medal Address 1988*).

Richard Meier Architect 2, Rizzoli, New York 1991 (Preface by R. Meier; K. Frampton, *Works in Transition*; J. Rykwert, *The Second Installment*; Afterword by F. Stella).

The Getty Center Design Process, The J. Paul Getty Trust, Los Angeles 1991 (Introduction by H. Williams; B. Lacy, *The Architect Selection and Design*; S.D. Rountree, *The Architectural Program*; R. Meier, *The Design Process*).

M. Brawne, *Architecture in Detail: Museum für Kunsthandwerk*, Phaidon Press, London 1992.

Five Architects/Twenty Years Later, University of Maryland, Fall 1992 (Introduction by S.W. Hurtt; K. Frampton, *The Five After Twenty-Five: An Assessment*; R. Bennett, *Recollections*).

G. Staal, *KNP Corporate Office Hilversum*, KNP, The Netherlands, June 1992.
S. Barthelmess, *Richard Meier, Collagen*, Germany, International Creative Management, March 1993 (S. Barthelmess, *The Collage in the Square: Art Parallel to Architecture*).
W. Blaser, *Weishaupt Forum/Richard Meier*, Max Weishaupt, Schwendi 1993 (Introduction by R. Meier and an essay by C. Rudeck).
P. Ciorra, *Richard Meier*, Electa, Milan 1993 (L. Sacchi, *Richard Meier o la rappresentazione della modernità*).
Meier/Stella – Arte e Architettura, Electa, Milan 1993.
Richard Meier, *Stadthaus Ulm*, International Creative Management, 1993 (D. Galloway, *Richard Meier and the Urban Context*; S. Barthelmess, *The Urbanization of Architecture*).
L. Nesbitt, *Richard Meier Sculpture: 1992-1994*, Rizzoli, New York 1994.
M. Sack, *Richard Meier Stadthaus Ulm*, Axel Menges, Stuttgart 1994.
S. Cassarà, *Richard Meier*, Zanichelli, Bologna 1995.
S. Cassarà, *Richard Meier – Works and Projects*, Gustavo Gili, Barcelona 1995.
R. Jodidio, *Meier*, Benedikt Taschen, Cologne 1995.
Stadhuis Bibliotheek: The city hall / library complex by Richard Meier in The Hague, NAi Publishers, Rotterdam 1995 (Interview of Richard Meier; F. Feddes, *The quest for the city hall*; V. Freijser, *The city hall as a pivot of urban renewal*;

O. Koekebakker, *A public library in a prominent place*; E. Melet, *The atrium, livable climate and technology*).
W. Blaser, *Richard Meier Details*, Birkhäuser Verlag, Basel 1996.
L. Fernandez-Galiano, *Arquitectura Viva Monografias 59: Richard Meier in Europe*, May-June 1996 (J. Sainz, *Houses and Museums: Meier in America*; T. Alezander, *L. Lefaivre*, *A European America*; J. Giovannini, *Modern or Contemporary*; S. Barthelmess, *Transparency and Perspective*).
New Buildings by Richard Meier, Architecture, February 1996 (J. Giovannini, *Is Richard Meier Really Modern?*, J. Giovannini, *Sculptural Sanctum*; P. Buchanan, *Aloof Abstraction*; M. Filler, *The Getty Gets Ready*; R. Kroloff, *Swiss Precision*; C. Davies, *Dutch Modern*; R. Barreneche, *Meier's White Turns Green*).
Richard Meier Houses, Rizzoli, New York, 1996.
I. Flagge, H. Oliver, eds., *Richard Meier in Europe*, Ernst & Sohn, Berlin 1997.
R. Meier, *Building the Getty*, Alfred A. Knopf, New York 1997.
Making Architecture, The J. Paul Getty Trust, Los Angeles 1997.
Richard Meier, Museum of Contemporary Art, Barcelona 1997; The Monacelli Press, New York 1997.
M. Brawne, *Architecture in Detail: The Getty Center*, Phaidon Press, London 1998.

A. Mulas, *Richard Meier: The Getty Center*, Poltrona Frau, Tolentino 1998.
J. Deal, *Between Nature and Culture: Photographs of the Getty Center*, Getty Trust Publications, Los Angeles 1999.
Office Building and Siemens Forum, Oskar-von-Miller-Ring, Munich, Siemens Immobilien Management, Munich 1999.
Richard Meier Architect, The Monacelli Press, New York 1999; The Museum of Contemporary Art, Los Angeles 1999.
Richard Meier Architect 3, Rizzoli, New York 1999 (Preface by R. Meier; K. Frampton, *Three Tropes in the Later Work of Richard Meier*; J. Rykwert, *The Third Installment*; Afterword by Arata Isozaki).
Italcementi Group, *Dives in Misericordia Church*, I, Project by Richard Meier, Edita, Rome 2001.
M. Daguerre, *Venti architetti per venti case*, Electa, Milan 2002.
Italcementi Group, *Dives in Misericordia Church*, II, Project by Richard Meier, Edita, Rome 2002.
V. Fisher, *Richard Meier – The Architect as Designer and Artist*, Edition Axel Menges, Stuttgart 2003.
Italcementi Group, *Dives in Misericordia Church*, III, Project by Richard Meier, Edita, Rome 2003.
Richard Meier, Electa, Milan 2003 (F. Dal Co, *Meier Style*; K. Frampton, *Forty Years of Practice*; *Works and Projects 1965-2002*).
*Richard Meier: The Architect as Designer and

Artist*, Rizzoli, New York 2003 (Preface by M.E. Shapiro; D. Shapiro, *The Song of the Object: Richard Meier as Artist*; V. Fischer, *An Emblematic Grandson of Modernism*).
Richard Meier: Thirty Colors, V+K Publishing, The Netherlands 2003.

Photographs
The Atheneum:
Ezra Stoller
High Museum of Art:
Ezra Stoller
The Getty Center:
Scott Frances
Canal Plus Headquarters:
Scott Frances
Museum
of Contemporary Art:
Scott Frances
Swissair North American
Headquarters:
Scott Frances
Rachofsky House:
Scott Frances
Islip Federal Courthouse:
Scott Frances
Neugebauer House:
Scott Frances
Chiesa del Giubileo:
Andrea Jemolo,
Richard Meier & Partners,
Alan Karchmer
Museo dell'Ara Pacis:
Richard Meier & Partners,
Federico Del Prete
Centro visitatori della
Crystal Cathedral:
John Linden
Sede Centrale Rickmers:
Klaus Frahm
Cittadella:
Richard Meier & Partners
173-176 Perry Street:
Scott Frances,
Zhonggui Zhao
Burda Collection Museum:
Pavel Stecha
World Trade Center
Proposal: dbox/Archphoto
66 Restaurant:
Scott Frances

Acknowledgments
We are especially grateful
to Lisetta Koe, Project
Editor, and Elizabeth Lee,
Communications
Coordinator, of the firm
of Richard Meier & Partners.